Down East They Say

Nancy Craig was
for many years at
Planned Parenthood,
where I knew her,
there after many years
as V.P. of hervey there
Hospital she moved (o
nox each yr) to Maine +
lived happily ever after

Collected Poems

Nancy Craig

First Printing

Design and typesetting: CMC Graphics, Crestwood, NY
Typeface: Book Antiqua

Distributed by New Highland Publications
newhighlandbook@gmail.com

ISBN   978-0-615-32269-8

Cover Art: Cynthia Hammett's *Down East Coast*; 2009
18" X 24" oil on canvas
Photo credits: Tom Arter

My gratitude to Harriet Sobol and the writers of 10 Claremont for helping me find my voice and for their encouragement.

To Doug, Tom, and Tim

CONTENTS

Brushstrokes of gold

Snow caking our lashes

This World

Where I live on mid-coast Maine
majestic pines stand high on the rocky ledges
oblivious to the drama of the crashing surf,
and the constancy of the ebb and flow of the tides below.

Lobster buoys in bright multi-colors
bob nonchalantly on the rippling water,
lie idly on empty traps and wooden fences,
fleck the scenic landscape.

I marvel at the wing span of the gulls.
soaring over fishing boats and white sails.
They call out —high, clear, disyllabic—
circle the shore before landing in berms of sea roses.

Down East folks with weathered faces,
wearing Bean boots, denim, and chamois shirts,
live in salt box houses and shingled capes.
They speed around in sturdy Volvos and Silverados.

They pray for sunny days and midnight showers
to nurture the lupines and blueberries and tourists.
Feasting on fried clams and boiled lobster, dipped in butter,
they fortify themselves to stay the same.

Down East they say, "you're from away," staring at my
Yankees cap and I ♥ Love New York shirt.
Redolent with conspicuous telltales,
I tell them, "Come, it's a great place to visit."

New life peeping forth

Mudscape

It's hard to feel glee Down East in March.
Late drifts linger in hemlock gorges,
the landscape is windswept —bleak, forsaken.

Up above, the pallid sky hovers over
gray granite, lapped by the restless sea.
Rain, like life leaking out, falls frivolously.

Mud has come with a vengeance
not caring what you think of it,
makes you ill at ease, mires your judgment.

Nothing's moving in the obdurate earth,
no pale roots digging down
or green shoots muscling up.

Melancholy silence lies end to end
past man's shadows.
I listen in vain for the jack-in-the-pulpits.

Spring's first inkling is the ladybug on my wrist.
It's too early to call it ebullience
but the red carapace seems pointed in the right direction.

*"If you have your debts paid, and made
your will and settled all your affairs...
then you are ready for a walk."*

Henry David Thoreau

The Walk

I've gone out walking anyway.
The stream I come to is slapping at the last
shard of ice that cracked off.
A sparrow's high notes from the bush
are chipping at it, too.
Crouched over, an old man sharpens his saw,
cuts lengths from limbs on the banks.
Not long ago the garden was humped by snow.
Now as I walk I can smell sod,
not the up-sprung smell of spring yet,
but a dank scent that heralds new life peeping forth.
I walk among the withered vines that withstood
winter and the fresh cattails, mulleins and flora
whose granaries feed spring birds.
The smell of balsam is bountiful
as I walk through the woods, green unfurling above me.
I feel the earth everywhere —a sense of God
alone on a leaf, in an opening bud—
something opportune. I keep walking.

Springtime

Winter, lean and naked, has silently slipped away.
Like waking from anesthesia, a new season stirs.
The flush of life is everywhere —forsythia flashing
brighter than pirate's gold, jonquils strutting in
synchronized harmony, the buds of dogwood
exploding in acclamation. Spring bids us to set free,
to become unanchored, to get ignited.
Throw open the windows and dangle in the warm breeze,
sing along with the larks stealthed high in the cedars,
dance bare footed on new wet grass,
feel the mist rise from under your soles.
Before the pageant passes like a parade,
before the blossoms fade and fall —run, laugh,
embrace the joy of it. Hurry!
Thus far all I've done is watch the weeping willows
where the river dallies by and
herons hunch in the blue billows of their wings.

Mother's Nature

Under a canopy of quiet pines
and fluttering poplars,
leaves unfolding pale green,
I pass through filigree woods
near McFarland Shore.

May's beauties, newly awake on the path,
lady slipper and purple violets
say, "Good morning," and
follow me to the old gray barn,
in the middle of the meadow.

She sees me first.
A redhead, eyes razor sharp,
charges through fresh blades
in my direction, head erect, body tense,
belly skirting the cool earth.

"Stop!" she glares like a sentry
guarding his charges.
I understand and step back.
Behind the barn, her six frisky kits
jump, leap, frolic —in utter bliss.

By Any Other Name

The well-placed stepping stones
take me down to the old brook
babbling through the delicate trees,
laden with dewy buds and
young pleated shoots.

Strands of rhodora illuminate
the water, casting a lilac haze.
Quirky jack-in-the-pulpit
and white-flowered bloodroot
elbow out the trillium.

Skunk cabbage, young and brash,
uncoiling deep veined leaves
as enormous as elephant ears,
show their sheaths near the traveled path.
"You're awesome," I whisper.

You wouldn't believe then
how the old brook starts roaring,
"Don't step on them."
Its memories of fetid odors fester
longer than the culprits it maligns.

What cruel curmudgeon I wonder
named this lavish lily nobody likes
except the skunk himself.
After all, not everything comes up
smelling like a rose.

Dining Out

The white jacket hangs loosely
on his broad shoulders.
He smiles —studies us
shrink wrapped in urbanity.
Cubes clink, clink
in the water he pours.
Where you folks from he queries.
New York we tell him.
His tanned face tightens.
"That's too bad."
He sets down the seared scallops.
"Been there —three times."
Blue lupine and sea spray
shine in his eyes.
"A shoe horn couldn't pry me from here."
He brings our sauvignon blanc.
"Born here —go to Bowdoin."
Maine is sublime we say.
With a big grin, he nods, pulls out the cork.

Sun slicing through

Three A.M.

For no good reason
I awaken from deep sleep
under dry eaves
and in the darkness
hear the passing night.

Enveloped in silence
I daydream with a black stare
and watch the restless sea
pounding hard blows on
the rocky headlands.

Frogs mating in the pond,
noisier than all get out,
have no regard for me or
the young doe dimpling the ground
as she dips her neck to sip.

I spot the wise old owl,
watch guard of the woodland,
high on the white bough of the birch,
his deft eyes darting back and forth
as the moon pulls him closer.

My head sinks deeper into the down.
I lie there minutes, minutes, minutes—
'til the bell buoys,
tossing and turning in the channel,
lull me back to oblivion.

Terra Firma

I saunter across Hillcrest's field
behind the renovated red barn.
It's a piece of ground I'd like to know better.
Someone patches the fence,
watches the weather come across it
day after day,
mows it starting in May and when snow is good,
might ski around its edges.
I walk down the long slope toward Back Cove —
the terrain lifts and hollows.
Like my gait, there's a spring to the turf.
I lie down and something in me
wants the firmness of the earth.
I look up at the sun slicing through the clouds,
watch the seagull's wings dip and pivot him.
The grass shudders slightly as a breeze passes through.
Then for some reason I start to remember
when I once lay on travertine marble
looking at the hues of the city sky,
and traced the tips of tall buildings.

An intrepid chipmunk scurries past me.
I wonder how it seems to him.

Sun Worship

White sands at Pemaquid glisten.
The Greek god near me
on the beach glistens too.
His well-toned body, coated with oil,
bronzes in the sun at high noon.
He lies comatose, flat on his back
with out-stretched fingers.

He doesn't know castles with towers
and moats rise all around him or that
a Lilliputian fleet of five sailboats has passed.
He doesn't see the gulls turning into small glints,
then nothing, as they climb higher and higher.
Deep in sleep, he doesn't realize the tide's coming in,
rippling closer, reaching his toes.

Leaping up, he drags his towel back to the dunes,
re-lubricates, turns over on his stomach.
He shuts his eyes and sleeps.
Aphrodite rises from the foam of the sea. Her long
hair moves toward him like reeds in the breeze.
They loll on the sand.
I watch in envy the grains rearranging.

Eye of the Beholder

Our guest from "away"
stands next to me on the foot bridge.
It's low tide. Before us fish houses
strewn with lobster traps line the shore.
Their naked piles, now tall as giants' stilts,
are laced with ribbons of kelp.

Sea life glimmers all around,
shimmers from the wetness
the receding ocean's left behind.
Millions of midnight blue mussels
blackened with microplants, slippery as eels,
anchor to the rocks by homespun threads.

Interspersed with leafy oaks,
balsam and pines crowd the banks
with lichen-covered dead trees—
some standing, some bent earthward,
others lying haphazardly
on the cool, mossy ground.

I smile unwittingly at the wonders of nature,
at the creatures that inhabit intertidal rocks,
the patterns of life before us,
salt water that flows in and out of the cove,
at an ancient world constantly creating, forever reacting.

Snapping out of my reverie, I look at
our guest, detached, his brow furrowed.
A laughing gull resting on the rail where he leans,
flaps its wings and flies off.
"I have no feelings about this," he says.
"We always went to the mountains."

Pounds Road Morning

At the crack of dawn the canis latrans
runs down our road
through the pinewoods pungent with pitch.

Ahead of us in plain sight, make no mistake,
it's a coyote in the flesh —pointed snout,
thin bodied, tawny in color, short haired.

His paws travel softly over the dirt and
tufts of grass. His long bushy tail
follows like a contrail.

He stops in his tracks, turns his head,
clamps his ice blue eyes on mine.
In the faint light, he looks deceivingly benign.

My terrier yelps. I pick him up, cover his muzzle.
Our hearts beat together like hammering waves.
We stand still, hear the chirping of the morning birds.

Just then the rising sun breaks clear of the trees,
drops its rays though the boughs,
over everything, over the coyote heading south.

After the encounter, the fear in my limbs lifts.
We brave the path —pick up our pace.
The dog starts to unwind. I slacken his leash.

Dru's Land

She lived next door on Pounds Road,
old Dru, who tended her acreage that grew by the sea.
Delicate and wan, her forearms lifted the chain saw,
its iron teeth chewing off limbs, truncating trees,
clearing the forest floor to let the light flow in.

Well into her eighties, in lush summer
Dru hurried between house and forest
on busy feet, which barely set down.
Making perfect piles of twigs and bark,
she named her tidied parcels "Betty's woods."

Oh, how we admired her passion, her resolve,
the satisfaction that bathed her face.
And when she went to her rest,
the birds on her branches chanted a requiem
that rose through the leaves.

Brushstrokes of gold

Equinoctial Sway

In September
when everything is rounding to fruition,
autumn touches me with brushstrokes of gold,
charms me with its allure, its beauty.

Before the garden fades like a dream
I write an ode to the Dahlias, large as saucers,
and the Morning Glory, lounging on the trellis,
opening and closing her lovely blue eyes.

Below the edge of the craggy ridge
the waves whirl in a crystalline spectrum —
azure, emerald, indigo, amethyst.
Before the breakers rest and the fog rises, I paint the scene.

At Back Cove, millions of black mussels
form a living mantle over the rocks.
Before high tide, I pull some off —hold them gently in my hand,
imagine the jewels that dwell within.

I stroll down the lane to visit the bold oaks
flinging their bronzed leaves to the wind.
Two ermine-tailed deer prance into the woods, like in a coronation.
I swing my knee over the stone wall —sit quietly, listen to acorns fall.

When I return you say the phlox need spraying,
cat briar's overrun the patch, branches laden
with apples bend pleadingly to the ground.
Help me bring in firewood and kindling, you say.

Not today. I'm savoring the sienna of equinox,
flocks soon to migrate,
the scent of first leaves falling.
I'm still reflecting —still absorbed.

New Harbor Hues

Spacious skies turn slate gray these days.
Woodlands with ripe decay stir uneasily in the raw wind.
The goldenrod whispers goodbye to
scarlet maples blazing against the church spire.

Beyond the ledges of granite, guarded by gulls,
the cobalt sea and harbor roil.
Lobstermen drop traps in deeper water —
work harder now for fickle returns.

Fathers and sons sharpen their aims
for deer and moose —for food and fun.
Reports from 30-30s puncture the air.
My white terrier, wearing an orange neckerchief, is crazed.

Saturday morning we go to the fair
where husbands show great pumpkins and
wives green tomato relish —everyone vying for victory.
Native grown apples and garlands of bittersweet line the stalls.

Back home we kindle the seasoned wood.
The kettle whistles quietly for afternoon tea.
We sip in the silence of late daylight,
acorn after acorn splatter on the deck.

Autumn sings a melancholy strain,
wants to stay on, to linger even longer.
It hardly matters if we give our consent.
Some will is done —past our understanding.

Seasons and Reasons

It's a still day —hardly a stem moving.
Chickadees eat seeds we put out,
the feeder swaying like a pendulum.
Birch leaves come down in ones and twos,
filling the eaves.
dropping amber dollops on the ground.

I stop daydreaming, mulch the lilies, write a poem, dig in.
Words come fast, then vanish.
I look up, relieved that nature's still there,
persisting in sublime indifference. Nature never seems to upbraid me,
needs no commentary like the new news blasting on the airwaves —
broken banks, bailouts, bad debts, tax breaks, bombs, boycotts.

I need a break and walk down to the water.
The red squirrel stops in his tracks
to see what direction I'm taking.
Daisies on the path are dead,
their golden petals shriveled up with grace.
Sea gulls fly off when I step on the whelk-riddled rocks.

Rhetoric of the human season rushes to my head —
semantic babble, verbal weaving, purple prose,
ballyhoo, nattering, mumbo-jumbo.
A hawk swoops down, narrowing the distance between us.
It braves its day with beak and talons,
whatever season.

Nor' Easter

The storm's face showed before I came.
They said it was blue and grainy.

Lofty spruce and fir all around
downed like columns of soldiers,
randomly dropping where felled
in woods, over roads, on fields.

Some saved and split
others pulled aside
most left in place to rot,
limbs rigid,
midst shrinking leaves
and luxuriant moss.

Turkey Trot

In the middle of the day
we walk among the seed heads
and dried stems
and the umbers of October.
Without warning,
a wild turkey runs across our path
through the shallow troughs
of casual water
pitting the old dirt trail,
through the pinewoods
on to Mill Road.
It's a "she" with a long neck stretched like a wind-flung banner.
Rushing somewhere
she trots off,
thinks no one has noticed her,
nothing except the sky
as clear as an undimmed eye.
My dog bounds after her —but
she disappears into thin air.

For Sale

At first I don't notice it —the "for sale" sign.
Standing on its runneled wharf,
the sun's tenderness on my face,
I see the old fish house in new light.

Weathered with character —quiet, aloof,
it sits there propped up by a single poplar.
Tufts of bearded lichen hang from the
branches like bits of sea mist.

The smells of old rotting nets,
brackish puddles in bottoms of skiffs
and the salt of the rimes that shines
on the rocks jolt my senses.

I fear the next owner will take an axe,
split the fused seams, discard the aged planks,
tear down the house —fecklessly.
The "for sale" sign looms larger than life.

The ocean, easing in and out of Back Cove,
day and night, rhythmic and insistent,
takes no position, sale or no sale.
Of this you can be certain.

Snow caking our lashes

The Pond

Daylight is breaking in full yellow and red.
I see that the pond froze last night.
Fallen leaves that floated at leisure,
are imprinted now, fixed in place.
The wind soughs and rustles in the pines,
its mouth whistling, blowing through me,
slapping my face.
My head sinks into my collar.
I look down on the smooth mirror
glazed with silver.
My foot touches the edge.
In the worst way I want to waltz across it,
be Sonja Henie, blond hair circling like a halo.
I worry then about skating on thin ice.
It's best to stand still —simply yearning—
this December morning.

Winter Mid Coast

Come to think of it, they'd warned us
it would arrive, undeterred —and on time—
floating in light as a feather, piling knee high,
with showy splendor, silent fanfare,
flake after delicate flake.

Bushwhacking scrub and brush, we stomp
through the woods, snow caking our lashes.
My pup roves ahead with ears pricked,
quivers like the frayed end of the drift,
wind blowing a rumple through his coat.

We don't see the deer standing
on the forest's edge, thin as rails,
nibbling their way across the peninsula, starving.
The pup sniffs the white air, burrows his snout
in fresh hoof prints, pounces in ecstasy.

When the hidden sun floats toward the horizon,
I wrap my arms around him
in the glistening snow. "We better go in."
The fire has died but the big clock
ticking loudly in the corner warms us.

Only half-asleep, we laze in our beds,
far away from the blazing white stars
and cold blanket covering the earth.
As morning breaks, we run out into the palace,
through deeply bowing trees, crowned in ermine.

Returning

From away we come early
in the new year.
Driving in daylight into deepening dusk,
night seamlessly comes.
We turn off 130 by the church,
go down the hill toward the harbor,
take the first right to McFarland Shore and the sea.

Since the new snowfall
our road is pristine white, untracked.
Dru's house ahead is a silent shadow,
looming in darkness behind the headlights' beam.
Outside the car, we hear only the crunch
of snow beneath our boots.

Inside the cool house, coats still buttoned,
we turn up the heat and light a fire.
The room is aglow with dancing flames.
I press my nose to the big black window,
feel the cool ocean falling on my face,
watch the stars burn on the water.
I'm stalled in the moment —then unbutton.

Choices

It's colder here than
a witch's teat,
bones chilled to the marrow,
breathe trying to get back in.

In white woods I walk
wrapped like Moscow,
tighten my wool babushka
stiff with saliva.

Pine gods beg me to stay.
I will I say
'til thoughts of hearth and hot toddy
wend me homeward.

With limbs stretched wide
I sit near the open flue.
The book feels warm
against my thighs still thawing.

"You're nuts up there," she calls
from her lanai down there,
nearly nude, fanning her face.
"Will it end with fire or ice?" I ask.

February's Man

After the snowfall he sees fresh tracks,
the leap of a hare, two black crows
perched on a limb.
Elated, he stands there
on the south slope,
his body round as the horizon,
spirits lifting in the frosty air.

The robust sort, he savors the elements —
the throbbing howl of wind
through the trees, cold against his face.
Shagged with ice, his felt hat
and red muffler glisten.
Plumes of smoke rise from his pipe.
He smiles at no one in particular.

For a week he's there —still like a statue,
ears and nose and fingers stiff as soldiers.
Then the sun leans down, blazing his heart.
Eyes coal black sink in, his pipe drops with a thud.
He falters, falls, shrinks —vanishes.
A silence slips around.
The snow starts falling again.

Canto 315

Rainy snow keeps coming
filling up the landscape,
usurping the soil.

We replenish the feeders
dangling on the gray branch.
Hungry, eager birds keep coming.

At winter's faltering end,
midnight digits keep freezing the
maple pails. Nothing outwits it.

The world, bleak and betrayed,
keeps wailing, weeping like
Lucifer —waist high in ice.

Opulent as a ruby, a small red finch
alights on the limb, sings divinely.
I feel a thaw —it's palpable and keeps coming.

A Predicament

She stands on Cunner Rock
a young woman
zipped up in royal blue
gazing out at the
never ending sea.

Other than gulls fluttering
around, scavenging for scraps,
she's alone there
with the lapping tide
and hovering clouds.

A lobsterman's woman,
hers is a tough lot, too —
briny and hard —brittle
as the shells feeling gritty
under her feet.

It's late but she dallies,
wooed by the water, stays
and wonders if another world
would goad her forward,
lift her to new heights.

The pupils of her eyes fix
on the gauzed horizon.
She cocks her head, listens for
an answer, but hears only the
discord in her heart.

The World Away

From "away," everyone's on fast forward,
busy, bustling, brassy.
New York and its suburbs burst at the seams —
a world where dreams are as lofty as its glass atria
and large granite towers.

Well planned streets lined with small trees,
sparkling with tiny lights, and urns of ivy,
pulsate with tooting traffic and flashing neons.
It's a world where gilt drips from vaulted ceilings and
sidewalk vendors sell Louis Vuitton fakes.

Citified folks in Burberry plaid and Armani black
speed around town in Ugg boots and tassled Guccis,
in hot pursuit of sea kelp and wrinkle-free faces.
Dining where Zagat rates, they feast on nouvelle cuisine and sushi
before curtain time on Broadway and concerts at Carnegie Hall.

Everybody "away" clings to iPhones and BlackBerries,
downloading the Dow and new deals in high definition.
When vacations are needed, they head for Tuscany, Vail and
even Maine. Down East they say, with its rocky coast, salt sprays
and squawking gulls, is picturesque —a great place to visit.

About the Author

Nancy Craig was born and raised in Madison, Wisconsin, and has lived all of her adult life in the East —Cambridge, New York City, Westchester County, Lincoln County. A former English teacher and retired non-profit executive, she writes prose as well as poetry and is currently writing a memoir of growing up in Middle America and a collection of vignettes called *Portraits*. A finalist in the 2008 and 2009 Greenburgh Poetry Contests, her poems appear in *Let the Poets Speak*. Her poems have also been published in the anthologies *Timeless Voices* and *Centres of Expression*. With her husband, Douglas, and West Highland Terrier, McFarland, she divides her time between their homes in Scarsdale, New York, and New Harbor, Maine.

About the Artist

Cynthia Hammett's adventures in art began as a young girl making shadow boxes, illustrating her autobiography and painting storefront windows at Halloween. But it wasn't until careers in corporate communications and journalism came to an end that her focus turned to her surrounding habitats on the coast of Maine, New York City and rural Tuscany and the painted canvas. Her work has been exhibited in Maine and Texas and is included in private and corporate collections throughout the United States, in Great Britain and Italy.

Printed by Lincoln County Publishing Co., Newcastle, ME